FATE

Books by Ai

CRUELTY · 1973

KILLING FLOOR · 1979

SIN · 1986

FATE · 1991

FATE

NEW

POEMS

Ai

BOSTON

Houghton Mifflin Company

1991

For information about permission to reproduce selections
from this book, write to Permissions, Houghton Mifflin
Company, 2 Park Street, Boston, Massachusetts 02108.

Library of Congress Cataloging-in-Publication Data

Ai, date.
Fate : new poems / Ai.
p.   cm.
ISBN 0–395–55636–8. — ISBN 0–395–55637–6 (pbk.)
I. Title.
PS3551.I2F38   1991   90–44251
811'.54 — dc20   CIP

Printed in the United States of America

Book design by Robert Overholtzer

BP 10 9 8 7 6 5 4 3 2 1

The poems in this book have appeared
in the following magazines:
Agni Review: "Jimmy Hoffa's Odyssey." *Alembic*: "Lyn-
don Libre." *Areté*: "Go." *Cafe Solo*: "The Cockfighter's
Daughter." *Chelsea*: "The Resurrection of Elvis Presley."
Hayden's Ferry Review: "General George Armstrong
Custer: My Life in the Theater." *Ironwood*: "James
Dean"; "Capture." *Manoa*: "Fate"; "The Shadowboxer."
Pequod: "Last Seen"; "Eve's Story"; "Evidence: From a
Reporter's Notebook." *Ploughshares*: "Boys and Girls,
Lenny Bruce, or Back from the Dead." *Poetry*: "Interview
with a Policeman." *Quarterly West*: "Reunions with
a Ghost."

FOR WILLEM DAFOE,

the muse this time

Author's Note

Fate is about eroticism, politics,
religion, and show business
as tragicomedy,
performed by women and men
banished to the
bare stage of their
obsessions.

Contents

Go · 1

Lyndon Libre · 6

Jimmy Hoffa's Odyssey · 11

Boys and Girls, Lenny Bruce,
or Back from the Dead · 16

General George Armstrong Custer:
My Life in the Theater · 22

Interview with a Policeman · 26

James Dean · 29

The Resurrection of Elvis Presley · 33

Last Seen · 37

Eve's Story · 43

Reunions with a Ghost · 48

Capture · 50

Fate · 54

Evidence: From a Reporter's Notebook · 58

The Shadowboxer · 66

The Cockfighter's Daughter · 72

FATE

GO

For Mary Jo Kopechne
and Edward Kennedy

Once upon a Massachusetts midnight,
under a sky smoothed of light,
as if wiped by flannel,
a car sailed off a bridge
but did not float.
Then the water, the dark gray water,
opened its mouth
and I slid down its throat.
But when it tried to swallow
the man they call my lover *and* my killer,
it choked and spat him back into your faces.
He carried no traces of me on his body
or in his heart,
but the part I played in his destruction
made me worthy of all of Shakespeare's villains.
Yet why doesn't somebody
tear me from the bit player's cold embrace
and let me set the stage on fire,
dressed up in revisionists' flesh?
Why doesn't someone write the monologue
that will finally explain this melodrama
and let me claim it?
Let me perform my own exorcism
as I performed the music of my dying
to someone else's rhythm.
Give 'em a show, Mary Jo Kopechne,

1

the one they really paid to see.
Bring down the house of Kennedy for good,
or, like Jehovah, re-create it in its soiled image.
I don't know. I don't know.
What scene is this, what act?
How did I miss the part where I enter to applause,
where the prince of make-believe
is waiting beside the hearse,
all its doors thrown open?
But right here in the script
somebody's written *Enter* beside the word *Exit*
and under that *You Choose.*
But when I do,
a human wall closes round me
and I can't get to you, Teddy,
behind your friends,
their arms raised to fend off blows,
even my own parents, with chests bared
to take for you any condemnation
aimed like a bullet.
If I shove those dominoes, will they fall
while I go marching in,
some Satchmo who'll blow the walls
of this Jericho of lies down?
But this aside's too complicated,
too weighed by metaphors and similes.

2

All right, I'll say it plainly.
Jack or Bobby would have died with me.
Think of publicity, the headlines —
you'd have been a hero.
Instead you caught your media resurrection
in your teeth and let it go.

You dove and dove
for that woman
so often reduced by the press
to just breasts and Mound of Venus,
but I broke free of all that.
I found another kind of ecstasy.
I'd always thought my only calling
would be acquiescent mate,
but goodness doesn't count
among self-made nobility,
especially the Irish Catholic ones.
What does is the pose of sacrifice,
so I swam deeper and deeper down,
hoping you'd understand and follow,
but each time you rose for air,
you sucked it like a child at breast.
It should have been mine,
full of death's sweet buttermilk,
but yes, you broke the skin of water

3

one last time,
you climbed onto Dyke Bridge
alive, but dead to the world.
If only you'd realized it.

How ironic that from your stained integrity
came the conscience of what's left
of the Democratic party,
brought to its knobby knees by Mistress Fortune.
You have earned that,
you who've grown fat and jowly
at the table where no feast is ever served,
just sparkling water with a twist of lime,
where once a glass of gin and tonic stood,
a good son's hands about to raise it in a toast
in praise of brothers.
Sometimes, stunned, you ask the dark
beyond the footlights
what happened to that life.
Other times, you slowly strip
to a Bessie Smith blues song,
you know the one about dues
and jelly, always jellyroll,
or you play the old magic trick —
a member of the audience holds up
an object from your past

4

and you identify it with charades.
But if you'd only ask me,
I'd erase those lines you've drawn on air
and deconstruct my own unfinished masterpiece,
a family portrait
of one man
and one true wife,
who, though the race was lost long ago,
stands behind him
with a starting gun
as he forever runs and runs in place.

LYNDON LIBRE

They'll chew you up
and spit you out, said Mother,
Mother said, but she was dead
before she saw the first red marks,
where the teeth bit deepest.
Praise God she never knew
that it would become patriotic
for quixotic Americans
to turn against their comet of a man
until, like wolves in dove's clothing,
they ran him down
on the steps of a white house,
the front door like that plywood door
of Reata Ranch in *Giant*,
opening on nothing,
though you all call it president.
In ancient times, a pharaoh
might sacrifice himself,
might through the shedding of his blood
save his subjects from drought,
disease, and other forms of tragedy,
until the ritual became
simply strapping on a panther's tail,
a symbol of renewal,
so when my falling came,
I pulled on my handlasted boots,

my spurs, Stetson,
chaps, and six-gun
and with a thunderclap
chose to ride the range
where only thorny, yellow roses grow
upon the once and future fruited plain.
Historians say that toward the end
I disengaged, even staged
my own tumble from the precipice called Vietnam.
I called her name in my sleep,
the black-haired bitch
who kept her knees together.
Whether I cursed, cried, or begged
she denied me,
and even when tied down and spread-legged,
she gave me no pleasure.
Defeat was the only treasure buried there.
Three days, I lay in Gallup's cave,
until the stonehearted populace rolled back
and I was saved by a cowboy all in black.
He gave me tobacco, hardtack,
two packhorses, and a map
and said, retrace your life,
and everywhere I set my feet,
my own face looked up at me
without a trace of recognition,

7

and only when I camped on the banks of this Mekong
of the mind did I find
I had not been erased.
Now I sit before the fire.
I swap tales with myself and sing
of herding human cattle endlessly
across the borders wars can always penetrate
but never quite make disappear,
while those who suffer fear, poverty,
race and class hate
are still outside barbed wire fences, iron gates,
anyplace but beside us at the table,
eating off our spotless plates.
I tried to change that
but could not break the locks
that kept me in the magic circle
known as the sovereign state.
My Great Society cavalry arrived too late
to deliver me from the calvary I had created
and only one man waited
at the foot of my rugged cross.
As I climbed down,
Bobby caught the dice I threw him,
blew on them twice,
tossed them, and said, "Luck o' the Irish."

Before they hit the ground, his heart exploded
and showered silver coins instead of blood,
yet cost me all a second time,
for martyrs never lose.
Blame my gradual disintegration
on intellectuals too,
ungrateful Negroes and the poor,
all beating at the door, until I bade them enter,
then found myself at epicenter of an earthquake
that still shakes the foundations of this country,
because in my wake came Nixon's Watergate
and later the final betrayal of FDR's New Deal,
·the ideology which now and then
Republicans steal
to accommodate the latest twists and turns
of their crooked highways.
But I know you'll cry
who am I to condemn,
who am I to say what price should be paid
to win and not.
If somehow the ends got mixed up with the means,
well, that's not communism, that's democracy,
that's the thin red line
between the white and blue.
I hope to God that will save you

from the politician's stew
of promises impossible to keep,
but me, I'm having barbecued spareribs
this Fourth of July, 1989,
pinto beans, corn on the cob.
At last I want to celebrate the brief time
inside the walls of Camelot
when I was king of comedy,
before I abdicated.

JIMMY HOFFA'S ODYSSEY

I remember summers
when the ice man used to come,
a hunk of winter
caught between his iron tongs,
and in the kitchen, my ma with a rag,
wiping the floor when he'd gone;
sweet song of the vegetable man
like the music
a million silver dollars make,
as they jingle, jangle
in that big pocket of your dreams.
Dreams. Yes, and lies.
When I was a boy, I hauled ashes
in a wagon,
pulled by a bony horse
not even good enough for soap,
so later, when they called me
stocky little dockworker
with my slicked-back black hair,
my two-tone shoes, cheap suits,
and fat, smelly cigars,
I didn't care.
I had my compensation.
Bobby Kennedy didn't want to understand,
but to the teamsters back in '58 . . .
I had 'em all in my pocket then,

statesmen, lawyers, movie stars,
Joe Louis, for God's sake.
For a time, I won spin after spin
on the tin wheel of fate,
but in the end, like those glory boys
Jack and Bobby,
I was only icing on the sucker cake.

I know the alibis, the lies,
stacked up like bodies
on a gurney going nowhere,
but Hoffa went, he went
walking in a parking lot one day,
while he waited for a so-called
friend, a peacemaker, ha.
See him there, bored and sweating.
See the car roll toward him
as he does a little dance, a polka step or two,
when the doors open
and the glare of sunlight off a windshield
becomes so bright
that he is blinded by it.
Later, I come to,
while a blue broccoli-looking creature
is taking tubes from my arms and legs.
Then he walks me round and round

till I can stand on my own.
He talks to me through some machine,
tells me I'm on a spaceship,
tells me he's lonely,
then he sits me down at the controls,
he talks to me about his life in some galaxy
whose name I can't pronounce.
I become a confidant of sorts, a friend,
until one day outside Roswell, New Mexico,
his skin begins to rot,
so I start collecting specimens for him:
rocks, bugs, plants,
my walks taking me farther and farther
till I find this abandoned gas station,
and when he dies,
I put up signs along the highway,
the ones that say, "10 miles, 5, 1 mile
to see THE THING!"
And fifty cents for kids, a dollar for adults,
buys a glimpse of a spaceman
in an airtight case
and Hoffa on the other side of the glass,
Hoffa who chooses to let everybody think
he was pulverized in some New Jersey nightmare.
I drink an Orange Crush, prop my feet up,
and watch the sun go down,

the moon come up. A year goes by like this,
two, when suddenly it's not enough.
In a rage, I smash the case
and burn down the shack
with the spaceman inside.
I hitch a ride to town and take a job
at McDonald's,
and when I raise enough cash,
take a Greyhound to Detroit,
but in the station,
as if commanded by a force outside myself,
buy a ticket back.
In the desert once again, I board the spaceship
and take off,
and one night,
kidnap two hunters in Maine,
later, a family in Texas,
a telephone lineman in upstate New York.
I want to tell them who I am,
but all I do is mumble, stare, and touch them,
as if I'd never been a man among men,
when the dollar sign was a benediction.
Instead of words what comes are images
of Hoffa smacked in the head
so hard he hurls himself forward,
then slams back in the seat,

14

and later, shot through each eye, each ear,
his mouth,
his body heaved in a trash compactor
and to its whir, whine, and moan,
crushed beyond anger.
Again and again, I play memory games
in the casino of the past.
Yes, half a chance,
I'd do it all the same,
so aim that pistol, wise guy,
and fire and keep on firing.
Let me go, let me go,
but give the bosses of the world,
the brass-assed monkeys
who haven't paid the price in blood,
this warning:
sometime when they are least expecting,
I am coming back
to take my place on the picket line,
because, like any other union man,
I earned it.

BOYS AND GIRLS, LENNY BRUCE,
OR BACK FROM THE DEAD

For Willem Dafoe, Ron Vawter,
and the Wooster Group

1

So how's it going, folks? —
broke, exhausted,
shtuped and duped again.
You can take it.
Hell, the meaning of life
is taking it,
in the mouth, the ass, the —
o-o-o-h
it feels so good.
All together now, stand up, bend over,
and say *a-a-a-h*.
Now sit down, relax, enjoy the show
that asks the magic question,
with such a stink,
can shit be far behind?
But no, what you smell is an odor
of another kind,
fear, disgust, plus all the things
you don't want to hear,
the things that drive you
from the club,
a body, a name, and nothing more.
Alone, on stage, I take

16

what you have left behind
and wear it like a wide, gaudy tie,
a sight gag
for the next show,
when I'll pick at some other scab
until it bleeds,
until that blood turns to wine
and we get drunk
on the incomprehensible
raison d'être of our lives.

2

I address myself
most often to guys,
because guys are least
able to express themselves.
You women know that.
You've read it in *Ms.* and *Cosmo*.
I am not a woman hater;
I'm a woman baiter, I like
to argue, I like confrontation
as long as I win,
but you women make it hard,
you don't play by rules

17

but by emotions.
One minute you're devoted,
the next you've placed
an ad in *New York Magazine*
that says we're impotent.
Know what I'm saying?
You women tell each other things
a guy does not want told.
You hold these secret sessions
over coffee and croissants.
We disappear in your complaints,
and in our places, those things
you've created.
So guys, I advise let 'em know
you won't be violated,
you won't be changed
into their tormentor.
You women out there,
all I'm trying to say,
in the end,
we're only bad impersonations
of our fantasies.
Just let the accusation waltz be ended,
not the dance.

3

I tried to reach
that state of grace
when performer and audience fuse,
but each show left a hunger
even sex couldn't satisfy.
The closest thing —
heroin. No,
like the Velvet Underground sang it —
her-row-in.
Shot, snorted, smoked,
even laced with sugar
and spread on cereal for breakfast.
But I was cool, it was cool,
until one night I thought
to hell with this moderation shit.
I took one needle too many
in that last uncollapsed vein,
that trail up the cold Himalayas.
I climbed and climbed
and finally it was just me
and the abominable snowman,
starring in my own *Lost Horizon*.
I had *arrived*
to Miles playing background trumpet.

Ice encased me from the neck down;
the snowman never moved,
never made a sound,
maybe he wasn't even there,
maybe he was the pure air of imagination.
That's o-x-y-g-e-n.
I breathed faster
and faster, then slow
and let it all come down,
but that was just before
the floor, the Hollywood
night and smog,
the quick trip to the morgue
to identify
someone I used to know.
He looked like me, he was
me,
but in some other form
or incarnation,
my rib cage cut open, my guts
bluish gray and shriveled,
liver going black,
heart too,
my dick sucked back inside,
as if through a straw or tube.
I lay like that for days

while they hunted me for drugs,
as if prospecting gold
and that gold was my disgrace,
but now I'm back
to claim my share of whatever's
left out there among the ruins.
And on stage,
under the white-hot spotlights,
give it all I've got.
So greetings from the reclamation zone.
Like Christmas, it was bound to come,
and like some hostage savior,
I'm here to stay
till everybody's sanctified
in laughter.
That's right, it's not your balls, your pussy,
or your money
that I'm after; it's your soul.

GENERAL GEORGE
ARMSTRONG CUSTER:
MY LIFE IN THE THEATER

After the blood wedding
at Little Big Horn,
I rose from death,
a bride loved past desire
yet unsatisfied,
and walked among the mutilated corpses.
Skin stripped from them,
they were as white as marble,
their raw scalps like red bathing caps.
Sometimes I bent to stroke the dying horses
as dew bathed my feet.
When I tore the arrows from my genitals,
I heard again the sound of the squaws.
The trills on their tongues thrilled me.
Those sounds were victory
and I was victory's slave
and she was a better lover than my wife
or the colored laundress
I took under a wagon one night
when I was hot with my invincibility.
Why, eventually even Sitting Bull
joined a Wild West show.
He rode a dancing pony
and sold his autograph to anyone who'd pay
and I might have become president,
my buckskin suit, white hat,

two guns, and rifle
flung in some closet
while I wore silk shirts
and trousers made of cotton
milled on my own shores
and took my manly pleasures
with more accomplished whores.
Instead I dress in lies and contradictions
and no one recognizes me.
All they see is the tall, skinny mercenary
with yellow hair
and blue, vacant eyes that stare,
so while I chew the tips of my mustache,
the cameras pass over me.
The journalists interview that guy or that one
and I want to shoot them down,
but that's been done before
by some back-door assassin or other
who kills publicly for sport,
but I kill for
the spectacle, the operatic pitch
of the little civil wars
that decimate from inside,
as in Belfast, Beirut, or Los Angeles,
where people know how it feels to be
somebody's personal Indian,

a few arrows, a few bullets short of home,
then left behind to roam this afterlife.
Once I knelt on one knee,
firing from my circle of self-deceit,
no thought but to extinguish thought,
until I brought down each brave,
but it was his red hand that wounded me,
no matter how many times I shot,
clubbed, clawed, or bit him,
my mouth overflowing with blood,
the rubbery flesh I chewed
that left no evidence of my savagery.
When I raised the gun to my own head,
I recalled the fields and fields of yellow flowers
that lit my way as I rode to battle.
How beautiful they were,
how often I stopped to pick them.
I twined them in my horse's mane
and in my hair,
but they were useless amulets
that could not stop my bullet
as it sizzled through flesh, then bone.
Now misfortune's soldier,
black armband on sleeve and hand on heart,
I pledge no fear

as chance propels me
into another breach
from which there is no deliverance,
only the tragicomedy of defeat acted out
in the belly of the cosmic whale,
where I swim against the dark, relentless tide.

INTERVIEW WITH A POLICEMAN

You say you want this story
in my own words,
but you won't tell it my way.
Reporters never do.
If everybody's racist,
that means you too.
I grab your finger
as you jab it at my chest.
So what, the minicam caught that?
You want to know all about it, right? —
the liquor store, the black kid
who pulled his gun
at the wrong time.
You saw the dollars he fell on and bloodied.
Remember how cold it was that night,
but I was sweating.
I'd worked hard, I was through
for twenty-four hours,
and I wanted some brew.
When I heard a shout,
I turned and saw the clerk
with his hands in the air,
saw the kid drop his gun
as I yelled and ran from the back.
I only fired when he bent down,
picked up his gun, and again dropped it.

I saw he was terrified,
saw his shoulder and head jerk to the side
as the next bullet hit.
When I dove down, he got his gun once more
and fired wildly.
Liquor poured onto the counter, the floor
onto which he fell back finally,
still firing now toward the door,
when his arm flung itself behind him.
As I crawled toward him,
I could hear dance music
over the sound of liquor spilling and spilling,
and when I balanced on my hands
and stared at him, a cough or spasm
sent a stream of blood out of his mouth
that hit me in the face.

Later, I felt as if I'd left part of myself
stranded on that other side,
where anyplace you turn is down,
is out for money, for drugs,
or just for something new like shoes
or sunglasses,
where your own rage
destroys everything in its wake,
including you.

Especially you.
Go on, set your pad and pencil down,
turn off the camera, the tape.
The ape in the gilded cage
looks too familiar, doesn't he,
and underneath it all,
like me, you just want to forget him.
Tonight, though, for a while you'll lie awake.
You'll hear the sound of gunshots
in someone else's neighborhood,
then, comforted, turn over in your bed
and close your eyes,
but the boy like a shark redeemed at last
yet unrepentant
will reenter your life
by the unlocked door of sleep
to take everything but his fury back.

JAMES DEAN

Night after night,
I danced on dynamite,
as light of foot as Fred Astaire,
until I drove the road
like the back of a black panther,
speckled with the gold
of the cold and distant stars
and the slam, bang, bam
of metal jammed against metal.
My head nearly tore from my neck,
my bones broke in fragments
like half-remembered sentences,
and my body,
as if it had been beaten
by a thousand fists,
bruised dark blue;
yet a breath entered my wide-open mouth
and the odor of sweet grass
filled my nose. I died,
but the cameras kept filming
some guy named James,
kept me stranded among the so-called living,
though if anybody'd let me,
I'd have proved
that I was made of nothing

but one long, sweet kiss
before I wasn't there.

Still, I wear
my red jacket, blue jeans.
Sometimes I'm an empty space in line
at some Broadway cattle call,
or a shadow on a movie screen;
sometimes I caress a woman in her dreams,
kiss, undress her anyplace,
and make love to her
until she cries.
I cry out
as she squeezes me tight
between her thighs,
but when she grabs my hair,
my head comes off in her hands
and I take the grave again.
Maybe I never wanted a woman
as much as that anyway,
or even the spice of man on man
that I encountered once or twice,
the hole where I shoved myself,
framed by an aureole of coarse hair.
By that twilight in '55,
I had devised a way

30

of living in between
the rules that other people make.
The bongos, the dance classes with Eartha Kitt,
and finally racing cars,
I loved the incongruity of it.
They used to say that I was always on
and couldn't separate myself
from the characters I played,
and if I hadn't died,
I'd have burned out anyway,
but I didn't give Quaker's shit, man,
I gave performances.
I even peed on the set of *Giant* —
that's right —
and turned around
and did a scene with Liz Taylor.
I didn't wash my hands first.
All the same, I didn't need an audience.
That's the difference
between an actor
and some sly pretender
who manipulates himself
up on the tarnished silver screen.
I didn't *do* method; I did James Dean.
Since then, the posters, photographs, biographies
keep me unbetrayed by age or fashion,

and as many shows a night as it's requested,
I reenact my passion play
for anyone who's interested,
and when my Porsche
slams into that Ford,
I'm doing one hundred eighty-six thousand
miles a second,
but I never leave the stage.

THE RESURRECTION OF
ELVIS PRESLEY

Once upon a time, I practiced moves in a mirror —
half spastic, half Nijinsky,
with a dash of belly dancer
to make the little girls burn.
I dyed my dark blond hair black
and coated it with Royal Crown pomade,
that stuff the Negroes used,
till it shone
with a porcelainlike glaze.
Some nights I'd wake in a sweat.
I'd have to take off my p.j.'s.
I'd imagine I was Tony Curtis
and I'd get a hard-on,
then, ashamed, get up
and stare at myself in the mirror by nightlight
and, shaking as if I had a fever,
step, cross step, pump my belly,
grind my hips, and jump back
and fling one arm above my head,
the other toward the floor,
fingers spread wide
to indicate true feeling.
But where was he
when I bit the hook
and got reeled in
and at the bitter end of the rod

found not God but Papa Hemingway,
banished too to this island
in the stream of unconsciousness,
to await the Apocalypse of Revelations
or just another big fish?

2

I don't know how it happened,
but I became all appetite.
I took another pill, another woman,
or built another room
to store the gifts I got from fans
till neither preachers, priests,
nor Yogananda's autobiography
could help me.
The Colonel tied a string around my neck
and led me anywhere he wanted.
I was his teddy bear
and yours and yours and yours.
But did I whine, did I complain about it?
Like a greased pig,
I slid through everybody's hands
till I got caught between the undertaker's sheets.
And now I wait
to be raised up like some *Titanic*

from the Rock 'n' Roll Atlantic.
Now as I cast my line,
tongues of flame
lick the air above my head,
announcing some Pentecost,
or transcendental storm,
but Papa tells me it's only death who's coming
and he's just a mutated brother
who skims the dark floor
of all our troubled waters
and rises now and then to eat the bait.
But once he wrestled me
like Jacob's angel
and I let him win
because he promised resurrection
in some sweeter by-and-by,
and when he comes to me again
I'll pin him down
until he claims me
from the walleye of this hurricane
and takes me
I don't care how,
as long as he just takes me.
But Papa says forget him
and catch what I can,
even if it's just sweet time,

because it's better than nothing,
better even than waiting
in the heavenly deep-freeze,
then he tells me don't move,
don't talk,
and for Chrissakes don't sing,
and I do what he wants,
me, the king of noise,
but in my memories
this country boy *is* singing,
he's dancing in the dark
and always will.

LAST SEEN
For Alfred Hitchcock

Good evening. I know you thought
you'd seen and heard
the last of me,
martini in hand
and vitriolic monologue upon the tongue,
not at all surprised to find myself
locked out of Paradise.
Why not? Consummation never lives
up to its promise.
Liver and onions with bacon
crumbled on the top
can serve you just as well,
whether you eat it
and/or hit your lover
with the skillet it was cooked in.
If the thirst for love
is not the thirst for death, what is it? —
a minute or two of heaving over the crapper,
a wipe, a flush,
a reverent hush before a scream
covers your body like a shroud.
Here lies Alfred Hitchcock,
a bloody nuisance
when he wasn't just a bloody bore.
He made films about unpleasant things and people.
He sold his name to magazines and television,

and some of you were patrons to his whores.
You cried, *Auteur, auteur,*
but all that ever mattered to him was the next scene:
a dark, deserted street, a large foreign car,
the camera far off, but moving nearer, nearer,
until the car's back end lifts slightly,
settles and shakes,
until I hear the muffled sobs,
the crack of a slap,
and a man snarling, *Bloody bitch. Bitch.*
Then silence as the camera moves back unsteadily
but suddenly goes forward again
to come to rest against the glass,
through which at last
by the unexpected flash of a match
I see his face,
suspended like a pasty moon
over the body of a woman
he continues to choke with one hand,
the sweat oozing off his rolls of fat,
as he wheezes and jerks
and with a groan ejaculates onto the corpse.
No, I'll not cut that bit from "sweat" down.
It's time somebody showed that side
of what is loosely called creation.
Wait. Wait. What if

a scant five minutes before,
we shot another window, perhaps catty-corner,
a convent window,
where a novice gazes down on the night
and its detritus,
on a blonde alone under a lamp,
beside a car
from which a puffy hand is extended
like a father's hand to a child.
She wants to *be* the blonde,
who's free to choose and discard
the rotten fruit of her desire
and in turmoil retires
to pray all night without solace,
while the other leans into the wide-open door.
Now fast forward
to the fat man on his knees, beside the body
he has just shoved onto the sidewalk,
grief and joy drawing him
down to the wide-open mouth, the purple tongue . . .
Cut! I cry
as I rise from my bed
and enter the other scene
that is shimmering before me.
Though the cameras keep rolling,
I wash off my leading lady's make-up,

unpin her hair.
She's wearing her seductive smile,
pearls, black taffeta, and Shalimar.
I run my hands over her breasts
and down her stomach
into the V where the hair must be almost white,
then I turn her over, lift her dress,
and start to slide toward nothingness.
I keep my hand over her mouth
until I feel her body slacken,
and when I take my hand away,
a growl foams up her throat,
then I'm slamming against the door
she kept locked so long
until it cracks and caves in.
But she's gone.
On the vanity, a tube of Love That Red,
a cake of pale pink powder,
and scribbled across the mirror

     No regrets

      G

As always, she abandons me
at the scene of a crime of passion,

but this time
I fit the chalk outline on the floor perfectly,
and it's my blood
gushing from a neck wound,
my blood, not hers, splashed over the set,
as if some imitation Jackson Pollock
had flung it against the cardboard walls
and called it art.
How it spills into the pristine
aisles of the theater,
only to coagulate at the feet of the murderer,
who's seated in the first row,
throwing candy wrappers and popcorn.
He wears the bow tie of clean conscience,
the wingtips of respectability,
the frayed charm of an aging boy
so well nobody suspects him,
not the mayor,
or the ladies in floral print dresses,
leaning forward in their seats
like wilted bouquets.
Finally, our exchange of identities is complete,
but now he doesn't want it.
He wants his silent witness back
and suddenly leaps up

and runs into the screen.
With a kiss, he resurrects me.
My double, my failed indemnity
against the starved, merciless self, I say
as I raise my hands to his neck
and squeeze.

EVE'S STORY

One Sunday morning Mama-cat
gave birth to a kitten
with no front legs.
Daddy was just a mouthful of Alabama dust,
but he had strength enough
to twist the kitten's head clean off.
The body was still soft and spongy
when I buried it.
I was sixteen. I left behind my cat,
my sister, and a ragdoll
when I ran down the empty road,
and I didn't stop
until I came to a tent set up in a cotton field.
When the evangelist looked up from the pulpit,
I saw his eyes were the size of blue glass dimes.
That night I joined his pitiful crusade.
I want you to understand
I made my sacrifices willingly,
because no matter what you think,
he didn't believe any less in Jesus
with a whore's titties in his hands,
with her hands pulling and jerking him,
until he shot his seed in a white handkerchief.
Afterwards, we'd pray together, the three of us,
before a painting of the Crucifixion.
Then he'd drive her to some corner

43

or motel, come back,
and rest his head on my bosom
and call me sweet sister, sweet,
until he met that "decent" girl in Galveston.
When finally he could not stop himself,
I taped her mouth, I held her legs,
while he shuddered inside her.
Later, he was so terrified by what he'd done,
I even had to zip his pants.
Then I watched as he apologized to her
on his knees.
"Please," he begged, drawing out the -*ease*,
"honey, please."
I said he couldn't help it,
it was my cross
and I bore it out of love.
After all, he'd taught me how to read and write.
She believed it. She was the type —
a white-faced cow
underneath the make-up and Neiman Marcus cloth
When we packed up, she followed us.
I'd go out and get his whores for him
and she'd join them
while I drank Scotch on the rocks
and read *TV Guide* or did crosswords.
Then I'd drive the whores

back into their ratholes
while the reverend and his press secretary
squabbled about his image. We had gone video,
but I wasn't in them.
I did not fit his image anymore.
Cheryl did, with her blue contacts, blonde hair,
and silicone implants.
I don't remember when I decided.
It wasn't jealousy, nor wanting to do right,
though I pretend it was.
That's too simple.
If they had known about the film I'd make
that one night,
would it have mattered?
When the first call came,
he didn't believe it,
and it was too late when he did.
Everyone began to desert him
while he stayed in his room,
watching the video over and over.
At last, even Cheryl told all on a talk show.
She got an agent, a book contract,
a condo in Beverly Hills,
where celebrities go to party
and complain
about how "rough the public is on us."

We lost everything, of course;
I mean, he did.
I'd saved up for my old age,
so now we live like any other
retired couple in Sarasota,
but we don't socialize.
Cheryl keeps in touch,
and now and then when she's down this way,
we meet for lunch
and don't know what to say to each other,
like sisters who once
had so much in common
but now have nothing but blood between them.
Before our meetings end,
she always takes my hand
and says, "You are a saint,"
then she rises and goes teetering off
on her spike heels,
though today, she does not take her hand away,
but holds mine down on the tablecloth
between the breadsticks and rolls.
We laugh, touching knees under the table,
then she hands me a packet of photographs —
first shot, the reverend, grinning,
as he jacks off into the camera's eye
and me overseeing it all

from my director's chair.
"If you hadn't," she says.
Of a sudden, I realize
this is how Eve must have done it.
The snake and God were only props
she discarded when she left Adam
writhing on the ground.
Once the scent of burning flesh and hair
pressed down upon her like a lover's body,
but now the smell of apple blossoms
hovered in the air,
promising sweet fruit,
promising everything we ever wanted.

REUNIONS WITH A GHOST

For Jim

The first night God created was too weak;
it fell down on its back,
a woman in a cobalt blue dress.
I was that woman and I didn't die.
I lived for you,
but you don't care. You're drunk again,
turned inward as always.
Nobody has trouble like I do, you tell me,
unzipping your pants
to show me the scar on your thigh,
where the train sliced into you
when you were ten.
You talk about it with wonder and self-contempt,
because you didn't die
and you think you deserved to.
When I kneel to touch it,
you just stand there
with your eyes closed,
your pants and underwear bunched at your ankles.
I slide my hand up your thigh
to the scar and you shiver
and grab me by the hair.
We kiss, we sink to the floor,
but we never touch it,
we just go on and on tumbling through space
like two bits of stardust that shed no light,

48

until it's finished,
our descent, our falling in place.
We sit up. Nothing's different, nothing.
Is it love, is it friendship
that pins us down,
until we give in,
then rise defeated once more
to reenter the sanctuary of our separate lives?
Sober now, you dress,
then sit watching me
go through the motions of reconstruction —
reddening cheeks, eyeshadowing eyelids,
sticking bobby pins here and there.
We kiss outside
and you walk off, arm in arm with your demon.
So I've come through the ordeal of loving once again,
sane, whole, wise, I think as I watch you,
and when you turn back, I see in your eyes
acceptance, resignation,
certainty that we must collide from time to time.
Yes. Yes, I meant goodbye when I said it.

CAPTURE

And that's how I found him,
hoeing weeds
in his garden.
He was shirtless,
his pants rolled below his navel.
I stopped and watched
as he swung the hoe down
to cut the head from a dark red flower.
He looked up then and smiled
and said, "It's like that with men."
He was not handsome;
his face was too flawed for that,
but somehow that made him beautiful,
with his thin hawk's nose over full lips
and the deep lines
that sliced his forehead.
His eyes gleamed
like two pale green chips of ice.
I said, "I'm a stranger here."
"You haven't seen our lake then,
shall I take you there?" he asked.
"When?"
"Now," he said, dropping the hoe.
He began to walk faster and faster
and I had to run to catch up to him.
There was no trail,

but he strode on through bushes that pricked me
and past low-hanging branches
that caught my skirt. Tore my skirt.
Then we were there.
"*Lake*, lake," I cried, then laughed,
threw my head back
the way laborers and drunks do,
and roared, or tried to.
"It's a pond for children to wade in.
At home, at home *we* have a lake
you can swim in;
it takes a whole day to cross it."
He stood with his back to me;
he was oily with sweat
and he shone like some living metal.
He turned to me. "Swim.
Swim?" he said with a question mark.
"I haven't got a suit."
"Ha!" he said. "Ha,"
and rolled his pants up to his waist,
daring me,
then lowered them all the way down.
I covered my eyes, and when I looked
he was walking into the water.
"Modesty, that's your name," he said
over his shoulder.

"And yours?" I asked.
"I don't need a name.
I am what you see."
He laughed and slapped the water
with his long, thin hands.
Then he swam from one side to the other;
he floated on his back
and I watched him, of course I did,
and when he was done,
he lay in the sun,
surrendered to the sun and my eyes.
"Do I pass now?" he asked
as he came to stand in front of me.
Then he said, "Seen one lately?
It's a fine one," he went on,
taking his cock in his hands.
"Touch it."
I shook my head.
"Get you," he said and began to walk off,
but I grabbed his hard, smooth calves
and kissed them,
and with my tongue
licked my way down to his feet
and kissed each toe.
He sank down beside me,
took my face in his hands,

52

and lifted my head back.
Then he kissed me;
our tongues battered our teeth. Touched.
He raised my skirt with one hand,
pressed me back
and held me to the earth
with the weight of his body.
I bit his shoulder
as he pushed into me again. Again.
I kept my eyes open. He did too.
He stared and stared until he knew.
"You tricked me," he gasped
as he poured himself into my glass
and I drank him like *grappa*
made from grapes
I'd picked with my own hands.

FATE

Sin must be cleansed by more and more blood,
as when the smooth, flat rock
the thin, pinched-faced antiabortionist
is hurling spins for a moment in midair
before it descends like Christ
into the body of a woman,
who cannot defend herself
against the judgment of men and God,
for we have always been the receivers
of what is given without love or permission
or whatever it is
that sends me to the well
as a Roman soldier gallops past,
dragging the body of a zealot
on a rope tied to his horse.
A swirl of dust rises skyward,
then a gust of wind blows it into my eyes.
First, a stinging that becomes an itch,
which radiates outward from my irises
like light from a star,
then Gabriel stepping from a golden cloud
to hold my head in his lap
and tell me how I must have the child,
that this shivering,
this heat and wetness
I feel between my thighs, is not real,

that he never lay beside me,
his robe open,
his man-thing covered by downy hair,
that I never pressed my mouth there
or felt him swell, or sat on him
and lifted myself up and down,
that this morning
as I plucked the Sabbath chicken,
the feathery touch below my navel
was just the spirit growing in me
and that the cry as I fell
with the jug of water was of joy,
the same joy I'll feel
when the head of the son who'll never be mine
rends my pelvis in two.

Now, who comes to me for advice,
who strikes her breasts thrice
to the ringing of bells,
as the smell of frankincense
wafts through motherhood's cathedral.
So many times, I've climbed
from my pedestal to stand among the protesters,
while the cameras beam another tableau of rage
onto television screens
like any other night's entertainment.

If I pushed them aside
to kneel beside the woman, who'd recognize me?
Who'd believe I'd forgive her,
for that is the province of men,
who condemn what they cannot abide.
It *is* true there are women who cast stones too,
but what if the price of their collusion
were infanticide?
What path would they choose then,
whose child abandoned
on some woman's Via Dolorosa
would they take into themselves
to swim the Fallopian tubes
to fuse to them and grow?
Are some children born to suffer,
because we say so?
If I hadn't let go my own son,
had held on to him only in the abstract,
not the fact,
maybe I'd have spared us all the decision
to have, or not.
I'd have stretched out by the table
laid with speculum, tenaculum, dilators, forceps,
the abortionist's humble tools,
to have my womb vacuumed as clean
as a vacated room.

Instead I lay down
in the blue abyss of His sacrifice
out of love and fear too,
the elemental kind that terrifies children
and those who send Hail Marys up
with the smoke of lit candles,
but Father nails them and their prayers to a stake
through their mother's heart
and departs to the sound of tambourines
and choirs singing,
ringing bells
and the crowd screaming *Baby killer*,
as I finally take my place beside the woman
and say my last Station of the Cross
to lost virginity,
the two of us a same-sex pietà of flesh and blood;
yet once we undressed by the failed light
of God and man's desire
and felt no shame
when He came inside us
with a ferocity that claimed everything we are
and remain.

EVIDENCE: FROM A
REPORTER'S NOTEBOOK

1

The city tosses and turns on the third rail
as the intern slams the clipboard on the desk.
He says, "We aren't finished with her yet."
"But Doc," I say, "maybe she's finished with you."
Schmoozing with an edge is what I call this.
He doesn't want the bruise of the six o'clock news
to blue-blacken his name by association.
He just wants someday to escape to a clinic
attached to a golf course
and drive his balls out
into the green bay it overlooks,
while back here, we all cook
in the same old grease
gone rancid from ceaseless poverty and crime.
"If I had a dime," he says, "if I had a dime . . ."
Then his voice trails off
and he stands and tries to swim
through the forty-foot waves
of three whole days and nights without sleep,
but each time, he's thrown back
on the hospital beach,
along with the dirty syringes, gauze,
and those who've drowned
in the contaminated water of their lives.

I say, "You know the hymn that goes,
'Some poor drowning, dying seaman
you may rescue, you may save'?"
"No," he shrugs, "it's more Charles Ives to me,
discord and disharmony
to go with all the inhumanity
that welcomes me each night
with open jaws and glistening teeth.
The victim, if she is one, is down the hall
and on the right. And this time, Maggie,
try to leave the way you came.
Don't make promises, or false claims of justice.
Let the lame stay lame,
don't set them dancing across the floor
in their own blood before they realize it."
"And what?" I say. "Go too far? But Doctor,
they're already there,
along with you and me, we need them,
they feed our superiority complexes.
You don't do Temple, I don't do Church,
but we've got faith, we're missionaries,
in search of some religion, some congregation
to place us in context,
even if it's someone else's.
And she *will* dance, as you and I will
and the TV viewers too,

to the fascinatin' rhythm of vaginal rape
and sodomization with a foreign object.
Hand me my tap shoes. I can't wait."

2

"You some reporter, right?" she says.
"It was a white man did this.
Said it is to show you niggers
who climbed from back of bus
to sit with us.
You nigger bitch, you get what you deserve,
and then he twist my arm behind me.
See the scratches, the splotches.
He drags me through some bushes and I got cuts.
You see 'em. You do.
He bit me too."
She tears at her skirt
and raises her knee, so I can see
high up her inner thigh,
too high, almost to knotted hair where underwear
of shiny fabric, nylon, I guess, begins.
"And when he finished with me," she says,
"he spit between my legs and rub it in."
I have learned not to wince

when such details are given;
still, I feel a slight
tightening of stomach muscles
before I make myself unclench
and do the true reporter thing,
which is to be the victim,
to relive with her again, again,
until it is my own night of degradation,
my own graduation from the shit to shit.
"Go on," she says, "write it down or somethin',
tape it, film it.
We got to hit him hard, hurt him. OK?"
"We will," I say, my smile in place now
like my hair, my friendship a brand-new dress
I wear until I wear it out or down,
but even as I take her hand extended to me,
so that we are banded together
in her stormy weather,
both without raincoats, umbrellas,
I flash on the report just read —
questionable rape, no tears, no bleeding there
or in the other place,
and bites that could be self-inflicted.
"Dirty sonofabitch," I say,
"is this United States of Revenge, or what?
We've got everything we need, got television,

and I have got your story
before the competition."

3

Six straight days, she's front-page news.
She makes guest appearances by dozens.
Everybody's cousin wants their piece
of tender meat,
but I've already eaten there
and I'm still hungry.
I'm suffocating too and I need air,
I need a long vacation from myself
and from my protégée
in all the ways manipulation pays,
when you play off the outrage
and the sympathy of others.
And she's a natural, she was born to do it,
should have her own byline in *New York Times*,
and I should have a Watergate,
should get my chance for Pulitzer glory,
but even Woodward faded like a paper rose
once he got his story.
I mean, you've got to know when to let it ride
and let it go, or else you wind up
some side show in Hackensack, or Tupelo.

You see, I couldn't prove that she was lying
and I couldn't prove she wasn't,
but that doesn't mean I abandoned her.
I swear the story led me somewhere else,
to the truth,
whatever that is, an excuse, I know, but valid.
Reality is a fruit salad anyway.
You take one bite, another, all those flavors,
which one is right?
She chose the role of victim
and for a while, I went along,
until tonight, when I look out
my window over Central Park
and think of other women whimpering
and bleeding in the darkness,
an infinity of suffering and abuse
to choose my next big winner from.
What I do, I take my own advice.
I whip my horse across the finish line
before I shoot it.
I step over her body
while the black sun rises behind me,
smoking like an old pistol.
The unofficial rules of this game
are that once found out,
you aim your tear-stained face into the camera.

You make your disgrace, your shame, work for you.
They don't burn bitches anymore,
they greet them at the back door with corsages
and slide them out the front into a reed basket
to float down the Nile, repentance,
into the arms of all us Little Egypts.
Welcome back.

4

My latest eyewitness news report,
focused on false accusations,
took as a prime example
my own delectable sample of the sport.
Even Warhol would have been proud,
would have remained in awe
long enough to list her name in his diaries,
might have understood her appetite,
have gained insight into her need,
though even her staunchest supporters
cannot explain away all contradictions,
all claims of violation that don't add up.
But really, if they only knew, in spite of that,
the lens through which we view the truth
is often cracked and filthy with the facts.
It could have happened. That is the bridge

that links the world of Kafka to us still,
the black pearl in pig's mouth
that won't be blasted out no matter what we do,
that finds us both on Oprah
or on Donahue, facing the packed pews
of the damned and the saved,
to send our innocence,
our guilt, across the crowded airwaves
to be filtered through
the ultimate democracy of TV,
which equalizes everything it sees
and freezes us to the screen between commercials
for movies of the week and shaving cream,
each show a rehearsal for the afternoon
when with a cry
she spreads her chocolate thighs
while I kneel down to look,
but still I find no evidence
of racist's or even boyfriend's semen.
I press my fingers hard against her,
then hold them up before the audience,
wet only with the thick spit of my betrayal.

THE SHADOWBOXER

You know what hunger is, Father,
it's the soothing half-dark
of the library men's room
and the reference librarian,
his head pressed against my thigh
as tears run down his pudgy face.
Sometimes I unzip for him
and let him look,
but never touch, never taste.
After all, I'm here to try to reconcile
the classics
with the Batman-comics philosophy of life,
and this pathetic masquerade,
this can't be life in caps or even lower case.
This is 1955, and all I know is boredom and desire,
so when I leave, I cruise down Main Street
for girls and a quick feel.
They call it the ugliest street in America,
but I don't know yet
that it's just another in a lifetime of streets
that end kissing somebody's feet or ass.
I just tell myself to drive and keep on driving,
but like always, I swerve into our yard.
You're still at Henrahan's,
drunk and daring anyone to hit you,
because you're a man goddamnit.

I climb the stairs to my room
and lie down under your boxing gloves,
hung above my bed
since your last fight in Havana.
When I can't sleep,
I take them down, put them on,
and shadowbox, until I swing,
lose my balance, and fall,
and on the count of six
you rise off the canvas,
only to be knocked backward into the ropes,
sure that half your face
flew out of the ring,
but it was only blood flung
like so much rum from a glass
into all the screaming faces,
into one woman's face
as she stands
and leans into the next spray of blood.
Do it, she cries
as she raises her fists, *do it.*
Bathed, stitched, and taped together,
you manage to dress
and get halfway to the street door
before you feel her
behind you in the darkness primeval,

but when you call, nobody answers
and you're twelfth floor up
Hotel Delirious
with Billie Holiday on the hi-fi.
Don't explain, she sings,
and the rum on the night table,
for the sweet dreams
it never really does bring, sings back, *Do*,
as you perform your latest attempt
to escape you, Father,
and what happened one night
when I stopped believing
even in the power of money to absolve.
Remember?
The first time I had a woman,
I even called your name. You didn't answer,
but you do answer the three short knocks,
and my mother, Rose,
still wearing her blood-spattered clothes,
crosses the threshold.
Turn back before it's too late, I tell her,
as she peels the tape off your face,
licks and kisses your wounds,
then mounts you
and plunges you deeper each time,

crying, *Show me what a good man can do,*
and you, Father, you,
rocking with her
until you must slow her, must ease her off
and stanch the blood above your eye.
Can you feel me, Father, breaking into a run
down conception road,
nothing but nasty business on my mind,
just two steps ahead
of all the bloody noses,
the broken bones
and blackened eyes you'll give me?
Nobody believes the lies you tell,
but they want to
and that's enough.
It's tough without a mother,
but fatherless is tougher on a boy, they say.
Nobody sees how twisted up I am
or how squeezed dry of anything resembling love.
I loved my mother,
but she left us to our few feet of deep space
for the hard chest and thighs of a comer,
the postcards she sent now and then from Venezuela,
Australia, even Paris,
reminding you of what you want to forget,

and when your good eye lingers on your son,
all you see is one more reason to hit him.

Then one night, you stagger to my room.
I don't resist when you slap and kick me.
Faggot, you scream
as you tear my T-shirt and shorts off me,
I heard about the library.
Then, then, you rape me.
You're snoring when I pack my gym bag
and take the boxing gloves
and stuff them in with my underwear
and Old Spice soap-on-a-rope.
I don't know where I'm going,
I just go as far as I can,
which in the end is Bellevue Detox,
is suddenly the smell of Gleason's gym —
men's sweat,
men's armpits, crotches,
men's wins and losses,
all that's left of Rosy Jack, Jack Rose,
middleweight loser
and sometime trainer of other losers mostly
or movie stars
and novelists who think the fights are glamorous,
who want to get in touch with themselves

70

by hitting someone else,
or for a "serious" role,
but I tell them
it's really all about a boy
finally beaten to submission.
Although he's crying *More*,
because he's been taught to think
he deserves to be punished,
he doesn't hear himself
as he locks the door
to keep his father in the wretched past
where he belongs,
but the past is now,
is you, Father, in this corner
and me in mine, stripped
to your level at last,
as the bell sounds
and the crowd bites down
on its collective tongue,
when the first punch stuns me
and the second knocks me all the way
to kingdom come and gone.

THE COCKFIGHTER'S DAUGHTER

I found my father,
face down, in his homemade chili
and had to hit the bowl
with a hammer to get it off,
then scrape the pinto beans
and chunks of ground beef
off his face with a knife.
Once he was clean
I called the police,
described the dirt road
that snaked from the highway
to his trailer beside the river.
The rooster was in the bedroom,
tied to a table leg.
Nearby stood a tin of cloudy water
and a few seeds scattered on a piece of wax paper,
the cheap green carpet
stained by gobs of darker green shit.
I was careful not to get too close,
because, though his beak was tied shut,
he could still jump for me and claw me
as he had my father.
The scars ran down his arms to a hole
where the rooster had torn the flesh
and run with it,
finally spitting it out.

When the old man stopped the bleeding,
the rooster was waiting on top of the pickup,
his red eyes like Pentecostal flames.
That's when Father named him Preacher.
He lured him down with a hen
he kept penned in a coop,
fortified with the kind of grille
you find in those New York taxicabs.
It had slots for food and water
and a trap door on top,
so he could reach in and pull her out by the neck.
One morning he found her stiff and glassy-eyed
and stood watching
as the rooster attacked her carcass
until she was ripped
to bits of bloody flesh and feathers.
I cursed and screamed, but he told me to shut up,
stay inside, what did a girl know about it?
Then he looked at me with desire and disdain.
Later, he loaded the truck and left.
I was sixteen and I had a mean streak,
carried a knife
and wore such tight jeans I could hardly walk.
They all talked about me in town,
but I didn't care.
My hair was stringy and greasy and I was easy

73

for the truckers and the bar clowns
that hung around night after night,
fighting sometimes
just for the sheer pleasure of it.
I'd quit high school, but I could write my name
and add two plus two without a calculator.
And this time, I got to thinking,
I got to planning, and one morning
I hitched a ride
on a semi that was headed for California
in the blaze of a west Texas sunrise.
I remember how he'd sit reading
his schedules of bouts and planning his routes
to the heart of a country
he thought he could conquer with only one soldier,
the $1000 cockfight always further down the pike,
or balanced on the knife edge,
but he wanted to deny me even that,
wanted me silent and finally wife
to some other unfinished businessman,
but tonight, it's just me and this old rooster,
and when I'm ready, I untie him
and he runs through the trailer,
flapping his wings and crowing
like it's daybreak
and maybe it is.

Maybe we've both come our separate ways
to reconciliation,
or to placating the patron saint
of roosters and lost children,
and when I go outside, he strolls after me
until I kneel down and we stare at each other
from the cages we were born to,
both knowing what it's like
to fly at an enemy's face
and take him down for the final count.
Preacher, I say, I got my GED,
a AA degree in computer science,
a husband, and a son named Gerald, who's three.
I've been to L.A., Chicago,
and New York City on a dare, and know what? —
it's shitty everywhere, but at least it's not home.

After the coroner's gone, I clean up the trailer,
and later, smoke one of Father's
hand-rolled cigarettes
as I walk by the river,
a quivering way down in my guts,
while Preacher huddles in his cage.
A fat frog catches the lit cigarette
and swallows it.
I go back and look at the picture

of my husband and son,
reread the only letter I ever sent
and which he did not answer,
then tear it all to shreds.
I hitch the pickup to the trailer
and put Preacher's cage on the seat,
then I aim my car for the river, start it,
and jump out just before it hits.
I start the pickup and sit
bent over the steering wheel,
shaking and crying, until I hear Preacher
clawing at the wire,
my path clear,
my fear drained from me like blood from a cut
that's still not deep enough
to kill you off, Father,
to spill you out of me for good.
What was it that made us kin,
that sends daughters crawling after fathers
who abandon them at the womb's door?
What a great and liberating crowing
comes from your rooster
as another sunrise breaks the night apart
with bare hands
and the engine roars
as I press the pedal to the floor

and we shoot forward onto the road.
Your schedule of fights,
clipped above the dashboard,
flutters in the breeze.
Barstow, El Centro, then swing back
to Truth or Consequences, New Mexico,
and a twenty-minute soak in the hot springs
where Geronimo once bathed,
before we wind back again into Arizona,
then all the way to Idaho by way of Colorado,
the climb, then the slow, inevitable descent
toward the unknown
mine now. Mine.